Contents

Language Arts

Social Studies

Mathematics

Science

Let's Go

Mrs. Cone's class is visiting the Green Botanical Gardens today. These words tell what the students will see:

workers	**squirrels**	**flowers**	**home**
father	**bugs**	trees	**park**

Nouns name people, animals, things, and places.

Read the sentences. Circle each noun that names a person.

1. Our teacher is taking us to the Gardens.

2. Two parents are coming with us.

3. A guide will show us different kinds of gardens.

4. All the visitors will have maps to use.

5. Write a sentence about the trip. Circle the nouns.

_____

_____

Try It!

How many nouns about gardens can you and a friend think of in three minutes?

These words tell what the class will do:

walk	watch	run	learn
talk	laugh	eat	sit

Words that tell what people, animals, and things do are **verbs**.

Read the sentences. Underline the verbs.

6. We're carrying our lunches.

7. Everyone climbs into the bus.

8. The driver starts the bus.

9. We wave good-bye to our friends.

10. Write a sentence about the trip. Underline the verbs.

_____

_____

_____

Word to Know!

A **botanical garden** is a special garden where plants are shown for visitors to enjoy. Scientists study plants at botanical gardens, too.

Try It!

Choose a story from a magazine. Read the story. Then mark the nouns with a pink marker. Mark the verbs with a yellow marker.

Getting There

A **map** is a picture of a place. This map shows the route from Perry School to Green Botanical Gardens. The **map key** explains the small pictures on the map.

1. Draw the shortest path from Perry School to the Gardens.

2. How many houses does the bus pass on its way to Green Gardens?

   _____

3. How many grocery stores?

   _____

4. How many gas stations?

   _____

5. Write two other places the bus passes.

   _____

   _____

Map Key

School

Shopping Mall

Park

Gas Station

House

Grocery Store

PERRY SCHOOL

Try It!
Make a map of your neighborhood. Show the streets, the houses, and the other buildings.

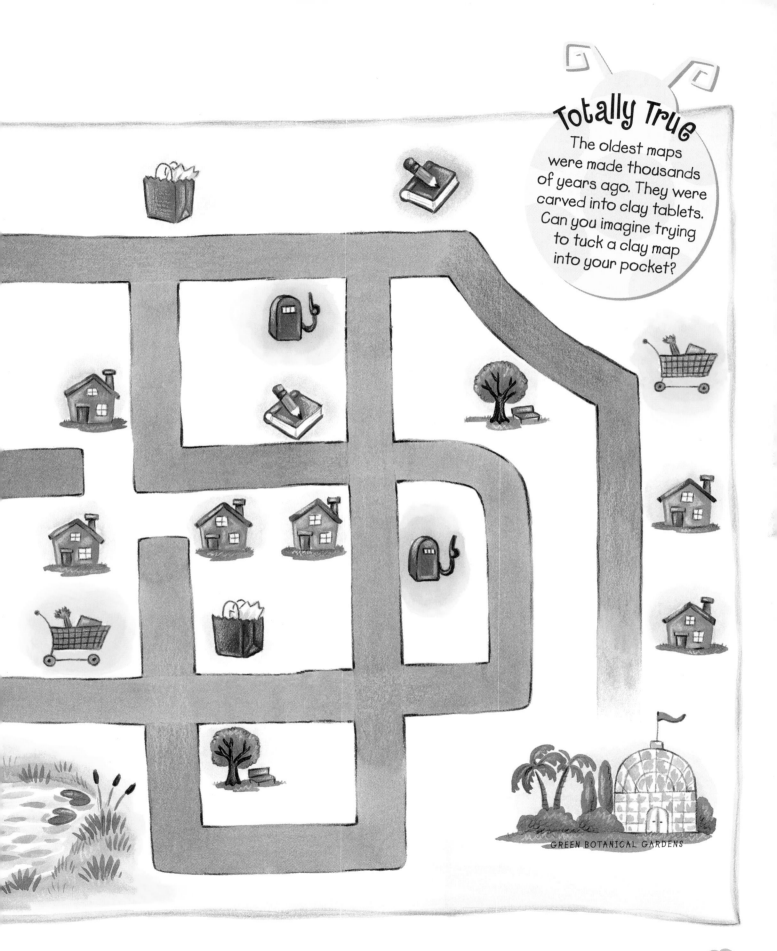

Totally True

The oldest maps were made thousands of years ago. They were carved into clay tablets. Can you imagine trying to tuck a clay map into your pocket?

GREEN BOTANICAL GARDENS

Ticket Scramble

The class is ready to go into the Gardens, but something has happened to their tickets!

Draw lines to match the ticket parts. Then write the sum or difference for each problem.

5-4=

10-5=

6+6=

5+4=

7+8=

8+3=

3-3=

5-2=

7+3=

9-7=

Totally True

One botanical garden in Hamilton, Ontario (that's in Canada), has a special 25-acre garden just for children.

Try It!

How many addition problems can you think of whose sums are 10? How many subtraction problems can you think of whose differences are 5? Write the problems.

Welcome to the Gardens

A **contraction** is a short way to write two words. An apostrophe (') takes the place of the missing letter or letters.

are + not = aren't   what + is = what's   he + will = he'll

The guide is talking to the class about Green Gardens. Write contractions from the box to finish the sentences. Below each sentence, write the words that make the contraction.

I'll	Let's	There's	I'm	We'll	Here's

DON'T PICK THE FLOWERS

1. _____ a lot to see at Green Gardens.

_____ + _____

2. _____ sure the class will enjoy our day.

_____ + _____

3. _____ what you will see today.

_____ + _____

4. _____ visit the rainforest and desert areas.

_____ + _____

5. _____ tell you about the plants there.

_____ + _____

6. _____ get going!

_____ + _____

Totally True
If there were no plants, there would be no life on Earth. The oxygen people and animals breathe comes from plants.

Try It!
Write three contractions you find in a book or magazine story. Then write the two words that make up each contraction.

What's in the Tree?

Juan has spotted a colorful bird in a tree. Would you like to see the bird's colors?

Color the **short a** words **red**.
Color the **short e** words **purple**.
Color the **short i** words **green**.
Color the **short o** words **brown**.
Color the **short u** words **gray**.

Turn the page upside down to learn what kind of bird it is.

Why do storks stand on one leg?

If they lifted the other one, they'd fall over!

egg
pet
red
went
mat
hill
lid
in
hop
dot
wing
snack
bus
rock
pit
up
block
back
pat
hot
sock
cot

Try It!

Write a sentence about a bird you've seen, or write about a made-up bird. Use one or two of the words in the picture in your sentence.

painted bunting

All about Birds

A **fact** is something that can be proved.
   Birds have feathers.
You can look at a bird or check in a book to find out whether birds have feathers.

An **opinion** is something that someone believes.
An opinion can't be proved.
   Birds are beautiful.

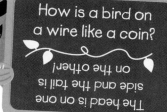

How is a bird on a wire like a coin?

The head is on one side and the tail is on the other!

Write **fact** or **opinion** after each sentence.

1. Birds have wings.

   _____

2. Birds help plants grow.

   _____

3. Everyone likes the birds at the Gardens.

   _____

4. Birds have bills and claws.

   _____

5. Birds fly too high in the sky.

   _____

6. Cardinals make the Gardens pretty.

   _____

7. Birds make the best pets.

   _____

8. Birds need food and water.

   _____

Try It!

Read a story about birds. Find at least two facts. Can you find two opinions?

Tweet Code

Add. Then write the letters to find out what the robin is doing.

p
```
  9
+ 7
─────
```
1.

e
```
  6
+ 5
─────
```
2.

i
```
  5
+ 3
─────
```
3.

s
```
  8
+ 7
─────
```
4.

H
```
  9
+ 8
─────
```
5.

g
```
  8
+ 4
─────
```
6.

c
```
  5
+ 4
─────
```
7.

r
```
  8
+ 6
─────
```
8.

h
```
  6
+ 4
─────
```
9.

n
```
  8
+ 5
─────
```
10.

i
```
  6
+ 2
─────
```
11.

		'									
17	11	15	9	10	8	14	16	8	13	12

Try It!

List all the addition facts for 9. Begin with 1 + 8. Then write 2 + 7, 3 + 6, and so on. Pair up the facts that have the same numbers, such as 8 + 1 and 1 + 8. What happens to the sums when you change the order?

Why do birds fly south in the winter?

Because it takes too long to walk!

Weather Watch

What's the temperature? Look at the temperatures at Green Gardens on different days. Write the number of the word that best describes each picture.

1. hot   **2. warm**   **3. cold**   **4. cool**

What was the weather like yesterday?

It was raining cats and dogs, and the street was filled with poodles!

Try It!

Keep a weather log for a week. At about the same time of day, write the temperature and draw a weather symbol in a notebook.

Words to Know!

The study of weather is called **meteorology** (mee-tee-uh-rol-uh-jee). A person who studies weather is called a **meteorologist**.

© School Zone Publishing Company

A Clean Scene

Workers and visitors help keep Green Gardens clean. They help **recycle**, or reuse, the trash.

Sort the garbage. On the line under each piece of trash, write the bin in which it goes.

1. _____

2. _____

3. _____   4. _____   5. _____   6. _____

Try It!

Next time you play outdoors, pick up at least one piece of litter and put it where it can be recycled.

Paper   Cans   Plastic   Glass

Subtraction Bugs

There are lots of bugs at Green Gardens.

Draw the other half of each bug. Write a subtraction problem that has the same difference on that half. Then color in the rest of the bug.

$$\begin{array}{r} 6 \\ -\ 1 \\ \hline 5 \end{array} \qquad \begin{array}{r} 9 \\ -\ 4 \\ \hline 5 \end{array}$$

$$\begin{array}{r} 17 \\ -\ 3 \\ \hline \end{array}$$

$$\begin{array}{r} \\ - \\ \hline \end{array}$$

$$\begin{array}{r} 18 \\ -\ 5 \\ \hline \end{array}$$

$$\begin{array}{r} \\ - \\ \hline \end{array}$$

$$\begin{array}{r} 12 \\ -\ 9 \\ \hline \end{array}$$

$$\begin{array}{r} \\ - \\ \hline \end{array}$$

$$\begin{array}{r} 18 \\ -\ 4 \\ \hline \end{array}$$

$$\begin{array}{r} \\ - \\ \hline \end{array}$$

$$\begin{array}{r} 9 \\ -\ 4 \\ \hline \end{array}$$

$$\begin{array}{r} \\ - \\ \hline \end{array}$$

$$\begin{array}{r} 9 \\ -\ 7 \\ \hline \end{array}$$

$$\begin{array}{r} \\ - \\ \hline \end{array}$$

Totally True
Gardeners and fruit growers love ladybugs. Ladybugs eat aphids and scale-insects that harm plants.

What kind of insect sleeps most?

A bedbug!

Try It!
Write all the addition facts for 10. Then write matching subtraction facts.

An Ento What?

Maggie knows a lot about insects. She wants to be an entomologist when she grows up.

Look at the creatures. Check the boxes next to the ones that are insects.

BUG FACTS

Head
Thorax
Abdomen
Wings
Hard Outer Covering
6 Legs
3 Body Parts

Words to Know!

Entomology (en-toh-mol-uh-jee) is the study of insects. An entomologist is a person who studies insects.

Try It!

Make a bug from materials you find around the house such as newspapers, bottle caps, toothpicks, and construction paper.

What is an insect after it is two days old?

Three days old!

Flutter Numbers

Count by fives. Write the missing numbers in the 100 chart.

5	10	15	20	25
30	35	40	45	50
55	60	65	70	75
80	85	90	95	100

Which number is five after?

25 _____

50 _____

80 _____

Which number is five before?

_____ 30

_____ 65

Start at 5. Connect the dots. Write the missing numbers.

30   35
40
46
25   65   60
55
70
15
135   10   5   25
80
125   85
110   90
115   95
100

Totally True

Scales make the pretty colors and patterns on butterflies' wings.

Try It!

Can you count from 50 to 0 by fives?
Can you count from 50 to 0 by twos?

Butterfly Sentences

A **sentence** is a group of words that tells a complete thought. A sentence begins with a capital letter and ends with a punctuation mark. This is a sentence:

    Butterflies like sunshine.

It tells a complete thought.

This is not a sentence:

    begins life as an egg

It does not tell a complete thought.

Use proofreader's marks to correct the sentences. Add words from the box to make sentences. The first sentence is done for you.

Proofreader's Marks

≡ **Make a capital.**

∧ **Add a word.**

⊙ **Add a period.**

| insects | butterflies | flowers | ~~begins~~ | kinds | fly |

1. <u>a</u> butterfly ∧ life as an egg⊙ __begins__

2. butterflies are __ _____

3. there are many __ of butterflies _____

4. __ live all over the world _____

5. they help __ become fruit and seeds _____

6. most butterflies __ during the day _____

Try It!

Draw a picture of a butterfly. Write a sentence to go with your picture.

Use a period (.) to end a sentence that tells.
Use a question mark (?) to end a sentence that asks.
Use an exclamation mark (!) to end a sentence that shows strong feeling.

Use proofreader's marks to correct the sentences.
Add words from the box to make sentences.

taste   who   defend   live   stink

7. Some butterflies __ only a week or two   _____

8. how can they __ themselves   _____

9. some make themselves __   _____

10. others __ bad   _____

11. yuck   _____

12. __ wants to be a butterfly   _____

Totally True
Learn to tell a butterfly from a moth.
• Most butterflies fly during the day; moths fly at night.
• Most butterflies have knobs at the end of their feelers; moths don't.
• Most butterflies have thin bodies without hair; moths have fat, furry bodies.
• Most butterflies rest with their wings up; moths rest with their wings out flat.

Try It!
Change an asking sentence from the exercise to a telling sentence. Change a telling sentence to an asking sentence. Write the new sentences.

Beehive Addition

Finish the beehives. Add the numbers across and down. An example is done for you.

15	2	17
3	3	6
18	5	23

1.
25	3
2	4

2.
5	0
21	6

3.
5	14
4	3

4.
34	3
12	5

5.
6	3
42	4

6.
17	21
2	7

Try It!

Make some addition beehives of your own. Make sure the numbers add up across and down.

Garden Rhymes

Words that **rhyme** end with the same sound.
The word **sat** rhymes with **mat**.

Read the sentences about plants. Write the
rhyming words.

1. Some plants have lots of spots.

   _____   _____

2. Some trees grow very slow.

   _____   _____

3. Some plants have ants.

   _____   _____

4. Some plants have bugs, and other plants have slugs.

   _____   _____

5. Some leaves blow in the wind as they grow.

   _____   _____

6. Some plants grow tall against a wall.

   _____   _____

Try It!

Play this game with another player. Make two sets of letter cards.

set one

| L | C | M | B | H | H |
| B | N | W | H | H | R |

set two

| and | ow | ame | ell | eat | ide |
| ap | and | ill | one | iss | un |

Put each set of cards in a jar or bowl. Take turns picking out a card
from each set. If the cards make a word, write the word. The first
player to make three words wins.

Totally True

Scientists believe
there are more than
350,000 kinds of plants,
but no one knows
exactly how many
kinds there are.

Leaf Pickup

The class is collecting fallen leaves. Subtract to finish the number wheels on the leaves.

1.

Wheel center: 12
5 7 3
4   8
9 5

2.

Wheel center: 11
9 5 3
8   2
6

3.

Wheel center: 14
9 7 5
4   6
8

4.

Wheel center: 13
4 7 5
8   9
6

Totally True

The sequoia trees of California are the largest living things in the world. They can grow nearly 300 feet high and as much as 100 feet around.

Try It!

Choose a number wheel. Write the addition facts to match the subtraction facts.

Write the differences.

1.
$$17$$
$$-\ 9$$

2.
$$16$$
$$-\ 8$$

3.
$$17$$
$$-\ 8$$

4.
$$16$$
$$-\ 9$$

5.
$$15$$
$$-\ 8$$

6.
$$14$$
$$-\ 9$$

In the Rainforest Garden

A **compound word** is two words put together to make a new word.

The **butterfly** flew around the garden.
Butterfly is made of the words **butter** and **fly**.

Read the paragraph. Underline each compound word. Then write the words that make the compound word.

When they got to the greenhouses, the class visited the rainforest area. Everyone looked around. They took their notebooks from their backpacks. Someone began drawing the banana plant. Somebody else asked questions about the plant.

1. _____ + _____

2. _____ + _____

3. _____ + _____

4. _____ + _____

5. _____ + _____

6. _____ + _____

7. _____ + _____

Try It!
Write a sentence about the rainforest. Use at least one compound word in your sentence.

Frog or Toad?

Fill in the blanks with words from the box. Then write the letters on the lily pads to find out what group of animals toads and frogs belong to.

smooth	land	bumpy	water	plump	hind

1. Frogs have long __ __ __ __ legs.

        1 4

2. Their skin is __ __ __ __ __ __ and moist.

     8

3. Most frogs live near __ __ __ __ __.

        5

4. True toads are __ __ __ __ __.

     2

5. Their skin is __ __ __ __ __ and dry.

     6   3

6. Most toads live on __ __ __ __.

        7

Lily pad letters: __ __ __ __ __ __ __ __ __

5 3 2 1 4 6 4 5 7 8

Try It!
Make a chart showing how cats and dogs are alike and how they are different. For example, both animals have fur, but dogs bark and cats meow.

Find the Pond

Help the frog find the path to the pond.
Start at 20 and count by 2s.

43	32	26	22	33	36	25	22	20	28
42	40	38	36	34	28	27	24	30	29
44	45	41	35	32	30	28	26	27	28
46	48	50	56	58	60	63	65	67	27
43	42	52	54	51	62	64	59	62	74
49	62	78	91	84	67	66	68	70	72
89	95	92	95	88	86	84	82	75	74
94	96	97	93	90	81	75	80	78	76
89	92	98	91	92	91	89	83	81	79
91	88	90	95	94	96	98	100	99	94

Totally True

A frog uses its long, sticky tongue to capture flies and other insects.

Try It!

Circle the tens. Then write the tens in order on a sheet of paper.

Rainforest Stories

Read about Green Gardens' rainforest area. Then answer the questions.

Martin and Lee saw something moving in the grass. They heard a peeping sound. The boys ran to see what was making the noise. The guide walked over. "That's a baby quail," she said.

1. What is a quail?

   A type of bird.

   _____

"This area had too many ants," the guide told us. "Quail like to eat ants. That gave us an idea. Now our problem is solved."

2. What was the problem?

   The area has too many ants.

   _____

3. How was the problem solved?

   _____

   _____

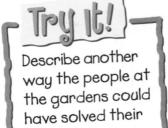

Try It!

Describe another way the people at the gardens could have solved their ant problem.

The guide showed the students some bamboo. Bamboo is a kind of giant grass with a hollow stem. Bamboo can grow more than six inches a day. Some bamboo grow as high as 120 feet. That's taller than 24 men standing on each other's shoulders.

4. Does bamboo grow faster or slower than most plants?

_____

5. What is one big difference between grass in a lawn and bamboo?

_____

In the tropics, or hot places on Earth, some people live in bamboo houses and use bamboo furniture. Their mats, baskets, animal pens, and boats are made from bamboo. Bamboo shades their yards.

6. Sum it up. Why is bamboo so important to people in the tropics?

_____

_____

_____

_____

Totally True

Pandas need bamboo even more than people do. Bamboo is the food they eat for breakfast, lunch, and dinner!

Try It!

Invent some other ways that people could use bamboo. Write two or three ideas or draw pictures to show your ideas.

Buy a Snack

Mrs. Cone and her students are visiting the snack bar.

Circle the number of each coin they need to buy the food. Use the fewest coins you can.

quarter = 25¢   dime = 10¢   nickel = 5¢   penny = 1¢

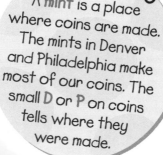
1.
45¢

2.
85¢

3.
69¢
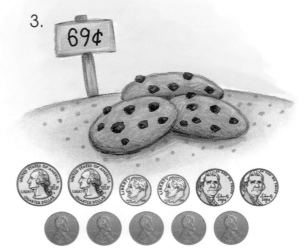
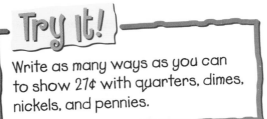

4.
$1.02

5.
$1.27

Try It!

Write as many ways as you can to show 27¢ with quarters, dimes, nickels, and pennies.

Resource Riddles

As the students eat their snacks, the class is talking about nature's useful gifts, or **resources**. They are discussing how to use the earth's natural resources wisely.

Write the resource after each clue.

| fish | water | trees | oil |

1. We use this resource for drinking, cooking, and bathing.

   _____

2. This resource is made into paper.

   _____

3. This resource comes from the ground and is used for fuel.

   _____

4. We can eat this resource.

   _____

5. We can swim in this resource.

   _____

6. We build houses and furniture with this resource.

   _____

Try It!

Write a way to guard, or **conserve**, each of these resources. For example, to conserve trees, you might suggest using both sides of sheets of paper.

Totally True
Wet your toothbrush. Then turn the water off while you brush your teeth. Turn the water on again to rinse. You've just saved as many as nine gallons of water.

Garden Time

Lots of things are happening at Green Gardens!

Draw the hands on the clocks to show the time of each event. Then write the time.

Green Botanical Gardens
Schedule, October 5

9:00		Snack Bar Opens
9:40		Garden Talk—Cactuses
10:45		Tour of Greenhouse
11:00		Class—Cooking with Garden Vegetables
12:30		Snack Bar Serves Lunch
1:30		Garden Talk—Taking Pictures of Your Garden
2:15		Cactus Committee Meets
3:05		Tour of Sculpture Garden

2:15

10 : 45

3 : 05

:

:

:

Try It!

Keep track of your activities for an evening. Write the time you eat dinner, do your homework, watch TV, and so on.

Cactus Subtraction

Find the differences. Draw blossoms on the cactus for the problems that needed regrouping. Are your answers correct? Check them by adding the answer and the bottom digit. An example is done for you.

```
  17
-  5
────
  12

  12
+  5
────
  17
```

2.
```
  13
-  4
────


+
────
```

1.
```
  26
- 15
────


+
────
```

4.
```
  18
-  7
────


+
────
```

3.
```
  20
- 13
────


+
────
```

5.
```
  56
-  9
────


+
────
```

6.
```
  70
- 27
────


+
────
```

7.
```
  55
-  6
────


+
────
```

Try It!

Make up two subtraction story problems about flowers using the numbers in two of the problems above. Ask a friend to solve the problems.

© School Zone Publishing Company

What's in a Book?

Kim and LaTasha want to learn more about cactuses. They choose a book about their subject. They read the contents page to find out what information is in the book.

Word to Know!

The parts of a book are called **chapters**. How many chapters are in this book?

_____

Contents

1. To which page would you turn to find:

   what kind of cactus the girls saw in the greenhouse?

   _____

   the name of the sharp parts of a cactus?

   _____

   how cactuses grow?

   _____

   another book about cactuses?

   _____

   how some cactuses are used in medicines?

   _____

2. What would be a good title for this book?

   _____

Totally True

Cactuses only grow a few inches a year, but they can live a long time. Some cactuses can live as long as 200 years!

Try It!

Go to the library to find books about plants that interest you. Do the books have contents pages? Read the contents pages. Which book would you most like to read? Why?

Put the Book List in Order

Help the Green Gardens' librarian. She has a list of new books. The list needs to go in alphabetical order by the title of the book.

Number the books in alphabetical order.

_____ **Mosses and Ferns**
      by Eugenia Charles

_____ **How Plants Grow**
      by M. E. Patinkin

_____ **Amazing Seeds**
      by Janice Carson

_____ **Plant Kingdoms**
      by Alice Addams

_____ **Wildflowers of Michigan**
      by Henry Spinella

_____ **First Seeds, Then Plants**
      by Gary Grove

Totally True

Some plants eat insects. Pitcher plants have tube-shaped leaves that fill with water. Insects fall in and drown. Sticky hairs on the leaves of sundew plants trap insects. Leaves of a Venus's-flytrap snap shut on insects unlucky enough to land on them.

Try It!

Can you teach a younger child how to put words in alphabetical order? You could use flash cards or a stack of books. Show the child what to do if the first letters of two words are the same.

The Garden Calendar

Green Botanical Gardens are open every month of the year. The Gardens are open every week of the year, but the Gardens are closed on a few days.

1. JANUARY
2. FEBRUARY
3. MARCH
4. APRIL
5. MAY
6. JUNE
7. JULY
8. AUGUST
9. SEPTEMBER
10. OCTOBER
11. NOVEMBER
12. DECEMBER

1. What month comes after:

   April?_____   September?_____

   December?_____   June?_____

   February?_____   August?_____

2. What month comes before:

   December?_____   May?_____

   January?_____   September?_____

   July?_____   March?_____

Try It!

Look at a calendar. Find your birthday. Write the month, date, and day (for example, May 3, Thursday). How long until your birthday?

What do you get when you cross a turkey with an octopus?

Enough drumsticks for Thanksgiving!

It's a Holiday

Green Gardens are closed on special days called **holidays**.

Write the letter to match each holiday to the reason we celebrate it.

A. We celebrate our country's independence.

B. We celebrate a leader who wanted all people to be treated fairly.

C. We celebrate the discovery of America.

D. We celebrate the new year.

E. We celebrate special friends.

What do you call a card from an animal with prickly spines?

A porcupine valentine!

☐ Martin Luther King Day, January 20

☐ Columbus Day, Second Monday in October

☐ Valentine's Day, February 14

☐ New Year's Day, January 1

Try It!

Look at a calendar. On a separate piece of paper, answer these questions:
- Which holiday will you celebrate next?
- What is your favorite holiday?
- Why do you like it best?

☐ Independence Day, July 4

What's Where in the Gardens

The **perimeter** is the distance around a figure. The perimeter is measured in units like this:

1 unit = •——½"——•.

1. Find the perimeters of the different parts of the Garden. Write them on the blanks.

2. Which area is the biggest?

_____

Now answer the questions about the shapes.

rectangle   square
triangle

3. What is the shape of the outdoor cafe?

_____

4. What is the shape of the orchard?

_____

5. What is the shape of the rose garden?

_____

How can you tell which end of the worm is the head?

Tickle it and see which end laughs!

Tropical Garden

_____ units

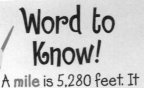

Word to Know!
A mile is 5,280 feet. It takes about 20 minutes to walk a mile.

Try It!
Measure the perimeter of some of the rooms in your house. Make a list of your results.

Apple Orchard

_____ units

Cafe _____ units

Rose Garden

_____ units

Why did the gardener bury her money?

She wanted the soil to be rich!

Try It!

Design a garden plan. Show all the areas where you would grow different kinds of plants. Label the areas.

Solid, Liquid, or Gas?

Think about it. Everything you see is solid (like rocks), liquid (like milk), or gas (like steam). Most things have only one form— solid, liquid, or gas. Some things can take more than one form.

Look at the picture of Green Gardens. Write **solid**, **liquid**, or **gas** on the lines.

Try It!

Try these experiments with matter:

1. Pour water from a faucet into a glass. What form does the water take?

2. Put some water in the freezer. What form does the water take?

3. Ask a grown-up to help you boil some water. What do you see above the boiling water?

How many forms can water take?

Fractions in the Kitchen

Cooks at the Green Gardens' Restaurant use fractions to follow recipes. Look at the fractions in the measuring cups.

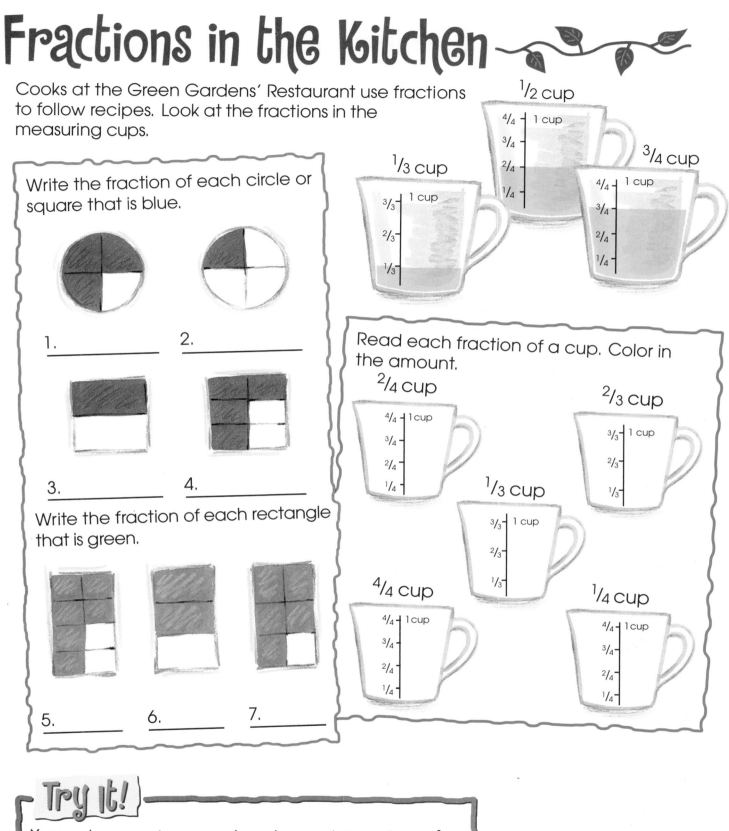

Write the fraction of each circle or square that is blue.

1. _____

2. _____

3. _____

4. _____

Write the fraction of each rectangle that is green.

5. _____

6. _____

7. _____

Read each fraction of a cup. Color in the amount.

²/₄ cup

²/₃ cup

¹/₃ cup

⁴/₄ cup

¹/₄ cup

A Plant Is Growing!

Some seeds grow into new plants. A seed bursts through its coat. Then roots grow down into the soil. A shoot grows up toward the sunlight. Leaves grow from the shoot. As the plant gets bigger, buds appear. The buds open up into blossoms.

A flowering plant is growing, but the order is mixed up. Number the pictures from 1 to 6 in the correct order.

Word to Know!

When seeds **germinate**, they burst through their coats and grow roots and shoots.

Try It!

Germinate lima bean seeds from packaged seeds. Wrap wet paper towels around the inside of a jar. Add water. Put the seeds between the jar and the paper towels. Leave the jar on a windowsill. Make sure the paper towels stay wet. In about a week, your lima bean seeds should germinate.

Lots of Seeds

You add **s** to many nouns to make them name more than one. Write these nouns in the sentences. Add **s**.

seed   coconut   dandelion   tree

1. Most plants grow from _____.

2. The soft white fluff on _____ is their seeds.

3. Some seeds become huge _____.

4. Did you know that _____ are seeds?

You add **es** to nouns that end in **s**, **x**, **ch**, and **sh** to name more than one. Write these nouns in the sentences. Add **es**.

wish   teach   class   bus

5. Green Gardens has _____ about plants.

6. Students take _____ to the Gardens.

7. My mother _____ she could come.

8. She _____ at our school.

Try It!

Read a story about seeds in a magazine or book. After you enjoy the story, see if you can remember two or three nouns from the story that name one. Can you remember a couple of nouns that name more than one?

Living Riddles

Plants can be tricky. Here are some ways they defend themselves.

Solve the riddles. Write the name of each plant. Use the pictures and words if you need help.

1. Ouch! Watch out for my spines.

   _____

2. I'm not poison ivy, but I'll make you itch!

   _____

3. People eat my fruit, but insects hate my citrus oil.

   _____

4. Prickles keep insects away from me.

   _____

5. Cut my blossoms carefully, or you'll prick your finger.

   _____

Word to Know!

The ability of plants and animals to blend with their surroundings is called **camouflage** (**kam**-uh-flahzh).

Thistle

Rose

Orange

Cactus

Poison Oak

Try It!

Look at a bird, squirrel, or other animal that lives near your house. How does the animal protect itself?

Garden Happenings

When rain falls in a garden, plants grow. Rain **causes** the plants to grow. The **effect** of the rain is the growing plants. Look for why things happen when you read. This will help you make sense of your reading.

Read each sentence. Write what is likely to happen, or the effect.

1. Mrs. Cone's class is hungry. Effect:

_____

_____

2. A very strong wind comes up. Effect:

_____

_____

3. All of a sudden, the temperature at the Gardens drops. Effect:

_____

_____

Fill in each sentence. Write what made things happen, or the cause.

4. _____

_____,

so people take off their jackets.

5. _____

_____,

so Mrs. Cone looks for him.

6. _____

_____,

so each student has a taste of star fruit.

Try It!

The next time you read a story, see how many causes and effects you can find. Write two or three examples.

At the Garden Store

Practice measuring. Use a ruler or trace the one on page 43 onto another sheet of paper. Cut out your paper ruler.

Guess how many inches long each item is. Then measure with your ruler to see how close your estimate was.

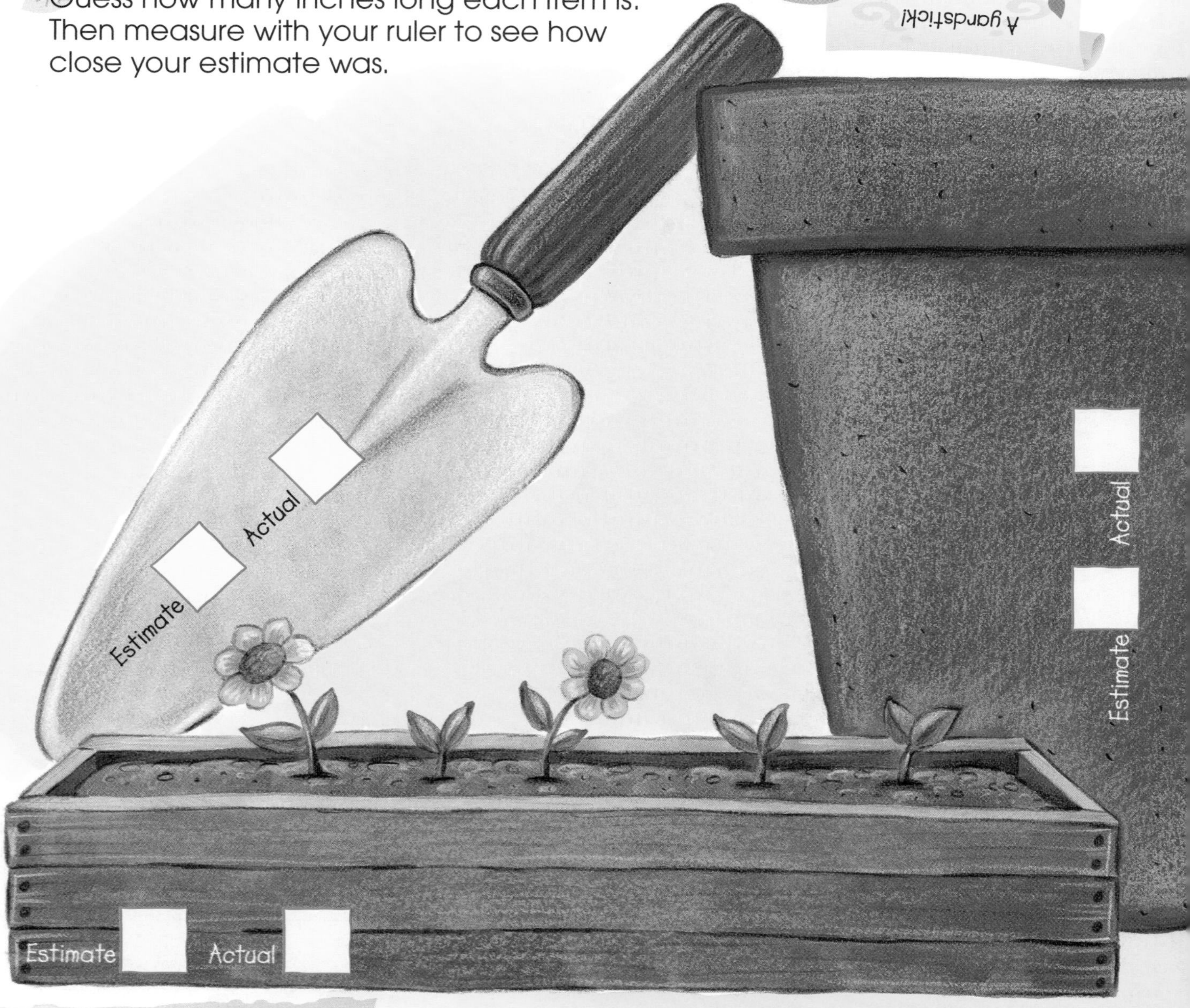

Estimate

Actual

Estimate   Actual

Estimate   Actual

Estimate   Actual

Words to Know!

There are 12 inches in a **foot**. There are 3 feet in a **yard**.

Try It!

Practice measuring some large things in your bedroom. How many feet long is your bed? Your desk?

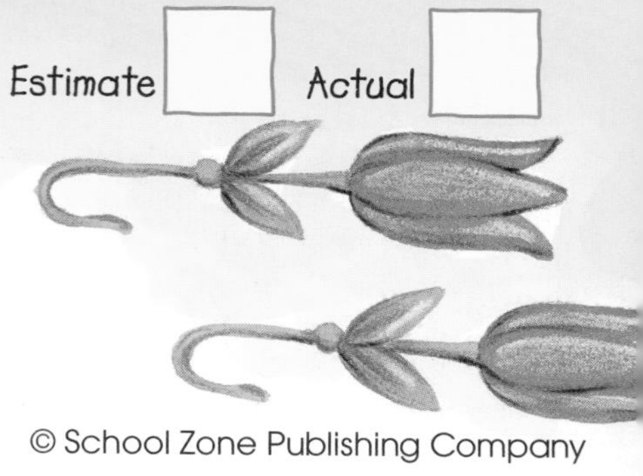

PERENNIALS

Try It!

You can measure with just about anything. Try measuring with paper clips. How many paper clips long is the longest side of this workbook? Measure some other things with paper clips.

Estimate

Actual

Estimate

Actual

Estimate

Actual

Estimate   Actual

Estimate   Actual

How much longer is the longest item than the shortest item?_____

Which things are the same length?_____

_____

What's It For?

The scientists at Green Gardens use many different kinds of tools. Here are some of them:

Scale

Thermometer

Word to Know!

A **seedling** is a very young plant that has just begun to grow from a seed.

Measuring Cup

Tweezers

Trowel

Tape Measure

Rake

1. If you want to find out the temperature, which would you use?

   _____

2. If you want to pick up some tiny seeds, which would you use?

   _____

3. If you want to plant a seedling, which would you use?

   _____

4. If you want to measure how tall a plant is, which would you use?

   _____

Try It!

What tools do gardeners use? Make a list or draw some tools and label them.

Producers and Consumers

Producers grow, make, or build things. **Consumers** buy or use **products**, the things that producers make. Every country needs producers to make things and consumers to buy things.

Look at the scenes from the garden.
Write **producer** or **consumer** on the lines.

1. _____

2. _____

3. _____

4. _____

Try It!

Write a paragraph about something you could produce. Who would buy it? What would it cost?

5. _____

Garden Code

Do you remember how to regroup when you add? Here's an example:

$$\begin{array}{r} \overset{1}{1}4 \\ +\ 7 \\ \hline 1 \end{array} \qquad \begin{array}{r} \overset{1}{1}4 \\ +\ 7 \\ \hline 21 \end{array}$$

Add the numbers. Then use the code to learn a plant fact that may surprise you.

LL	VA	OR	NI
29 + 3 **32**	18 + 5 **23**	15 + 5 **20**	17 + 9 **26**

A	S	CE	O
32 + 8 **40**	16 + 6 **22**	10 +14 **24**	17 + 8 **25**

DU	CH	PR	ID
15 +16 **31**	17 +24 **41**	15 +15 **30**	33 +17 **50**

or ch id s
20 41 50 22

pr o du ce
30 25 31 24

va ni ll a
23 26 32 40

Try It!

Think of a math code of your own. Write a message using your code. Ask a friend to figure out your message.

Bunches of Flowers

Some words have the same or nearly the same meaning. **Smile** and **grin** mean almost the same thing.

Draw lines to connect the pairs of words that have the same or nearly the same meanings.

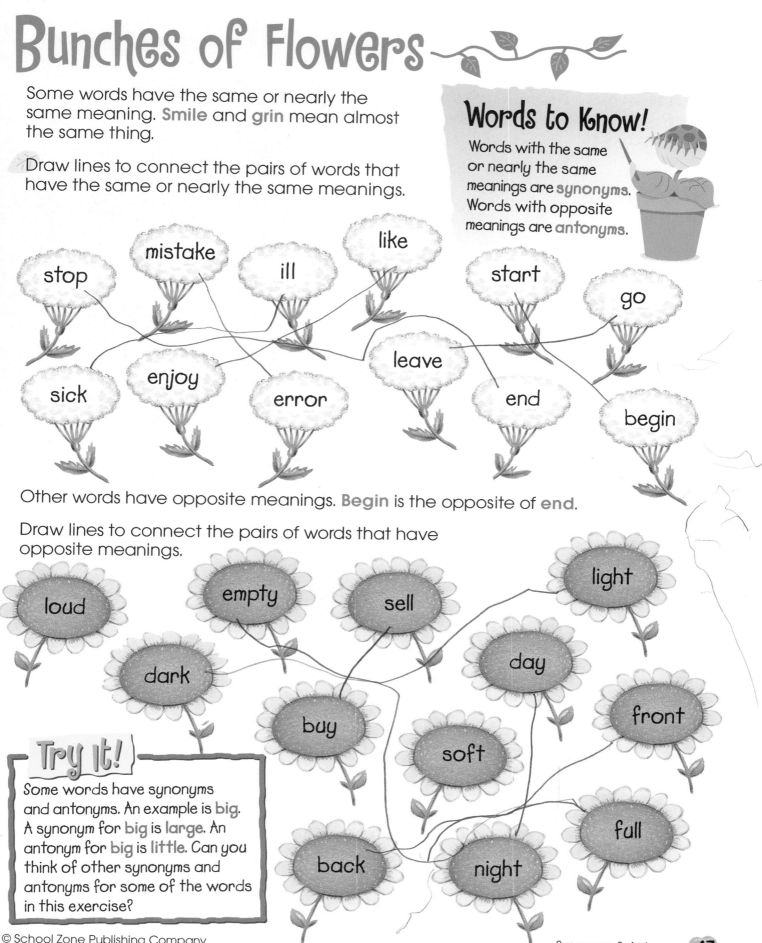

Other words have opposite meanings. **Begin** is the opposite of **end**.

Draw lines to connect the pairs of words that have opposite meanings.

Try It!

Some words have synonyms and antonyms. An example is **big**. A synonym for **big** is **large**. An antonym for **big** is **little**. Can you think of other synonyms and antonyms for some of the words in this exercise?

Timeline

A timeline is a good way to show when things happened. A timeline can show a day, a month, a year, or longer.

Here is a timeline of the children's visit to Green Botanical Gardens.

Words to Know!

A **decade** is 10 years. A **century** is 100 years. How many decades are in a century?

_____

Leave Perry School

Leave Green Gardens

9:00   10:00   11:00   12:00   1:00   2:00   3:00   4:00

Lunch

Snack

Add these events to the timeline:

• Tour Greenhouses 10:00

• Visit Library 2:00

• Arrive at School 3:30

Try It!

Make a timeline. You can show a day or week in your life, or you can show the most important things that have happened to you since you were born.

Be a Good Citizen

A good citizen thinks of other people.

Read the descriptions. Write **yes** if a good citizen does this. Write **no** if a good citizen does not do this.

1. helps others __Yes__

2. writes on library books __No__

3. drops trash everywhere __No__

4. obeys traffic signs __Yes__

5. runs in school hallways __No__

6. follows classroom rules __No__

7. Write one other thing you can do to be a good citizen.

_____

_____

Try It!

Add to the list. Describe what makes a good citizen at school.

Garden Books

Green Gardens' library has many interesting books for children.

Study the graph. Then answer the questions.

Number of Books in Library

	1	2	3	4	5	6	7	8	9
Roses									
Bulbs									
Cactuses									
Trees									
Moss									

1. How many books are about roses? _____

2. How many books are about trees? _____

3. How many more books are about bulbs than about trees?

   _____ ☐ _____ = _____

4. How many more books are about roses than about moss?

   _____ ☐ _____ = _____

5. Look at the books about roses and the ones about bulbs. How many are there in all?

   _____ ☐ _____ = _____

Wonderful Words

Some words have more than one meaning. A dictionary numbers each meaning.

Read the definition of **plant**.

> **plant** 1. any living thing that can make its own food from sunlight, air, and water. 2. to put in the ground and grow.

Read each sentence. Write the number of the correct meaning.

a. Where should we plant the rose bush? _____

b. The plant needs water. _____

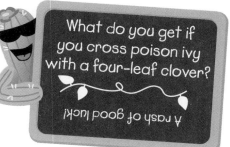

What do you get if you cross poison ivy with a four-leaf clover?

A rash of good luck!

Read the definition of **bulb**.

> **bulb** 1. a hollow glass light that glows when electricity is turned on. 2. a round bud or stem that you plant in the ground.

Read each sentence. Write the number of the correct meaning.

c. Oh, no! I think the bulb burned out. _____

d. Plant the tulip bulb in the garden. _____

Which trees clap?

Palms!

Try It!

When you come to a word you don't know in your reading, don't give up. You can skip the word and try to figure it out from the sentences that follow, you can ask someone what the word means, or you can look up the word in a dictionary. If the word doesn't seem very important, you can ignore it!

Garden Math Puzzle

Solve the problems. Write the answers in the puzzle.

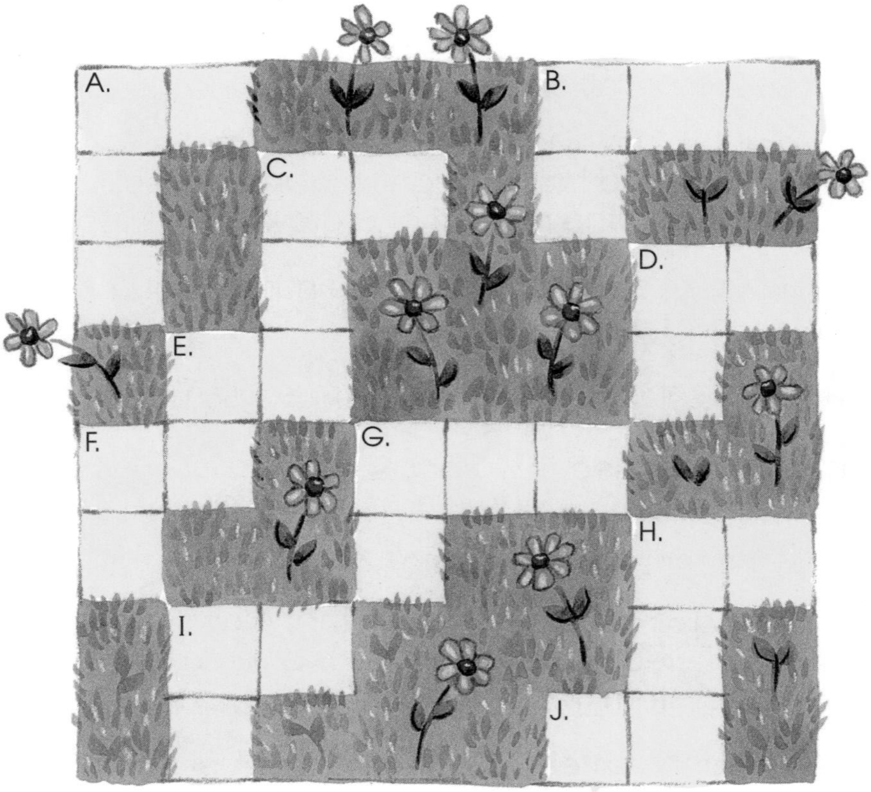

Across

A. 12 more than 10

B. 90, 95, 100, ____

C. 14 + 15 = ____

D. 8 + 9 = ____

E. 19 – 7 = ____

F. 3, 6, 9, ____

G. 120 – 15 = ____

H. 2 tens, 8 ones

I. 50¢ + 35¢ = ____ ¢

J. 29 – 13 = ____

Down

A. 284 + 12 = ____

B. 27 – 8 = ____

C. 2 hundreds, 2 tens, 2 ones

D. 5, 10, ____

E. one dozen

F. 2 x 9 = ____

G. 3 x 5 = ____

H. 2 hundreds, 3 tens, 6 ones

I. $1.00 – $.15 = $____

Try It!

Write all the numbers used in the puzzle on a sheet of paper. Put them in order from least to greatest.

What's the Problem?

Read the paragraphs. Answer the questions.

1. The class went to the gift shop. Reggie picked out a postcard to buy. He reached into his pocket for money to pay for it. Reggie looked surprised.

   Why do you think Reggie looked surprised?

   _____

   _____

   _____

2. Misty bought her mother a glass bird. When her mother opened the gift, Misty looked sad.

   Why do you think she looked sad?

   _____

   _____

   _____

3. Jill lost her purse. A call came for her from the lost-and-found desk. After Jill answered the phone, she looked happy.

   Why do you think she looked happy?

   _____

   _____

   _____

Try It!

The next time you watch a TV show, choose a character. Try to figure out why the character acts as he or she does. Do you know for sure, or do you have to guess?

Thanks, Green Gardens

Mrs. Cone's class is sending a thank-you note to Green Gardens.

1. To whom is the letter written?

   _____

2. What is the closing?

   _____

3. Who wrote the letter?

   _____

Write a letter to a friend about a trip you have taken. Look at the letter above to help you.

Date

October 5, 2007

Greeting

Dear Ms. Jones,

Body

Thank you very much for letting us visit Green Gardens. We enjoyed learning about plants in the indoor and outdoor gardens. We had fun collecting different kinds of leaves. We especially loved watching the baby quail run around.

Best wishes, **Closing**

Mrs. Cone's class

Signature

Activities to Share

Language Arts

Your Child—the Writer

Encourage your child to make up a story or recount an experience. As the "official recorder," write down your child's words. After the piece is finished, examine it together. Does your child want to change anything? Post the dictation on the refrigerator door where you and your child can reread it.

Develop Listening Skills

After watching a TV program or a movie, encourage your child to tell you what happened. These discussions will help develop your child's abilities to listen carefully and speak fluently.

It's in the Journal

Give your child the opportunity to write in his or her very own journal, perhaps a notebook for which your child draws a special cover. Tell your child that the journal may include pictures with sentences that accompany them, stories, or descriptions of daily events.

Taste the Stories

When you and your child read a book that involves food as part of the plot, sample the food mentioned in the story. For example, if you read Maurice Sendak's **Chicken Soup with Rice** or Beatrix Potter's **Peter Rabbit**, follow up by making chicken soup with rice or munching on garden vegetables.

Read the Signs

Have your child read road signs and the names of various businesses as you travel in your car. At the grocery store, encourage your child to read the signs to figure out which foods are found in the various aisles. Your child may also enjoy reading the backs of cereal boxes and milk cartons.

Read to Others

If your child has a little brother or sister or if there is a younger child in the neighborhood, encourage your child to read to him or her. Provide an easy-to-read book and let your child share the book with the younger child. Sharing books this way will build the child's confidence as a reader, as well as demonstrating the rewards of sharing.

Read, Read, Read!

Reading to your child frequently is the best way to make sure your child will be a competent reader—and one who enjoys reading. You may want to pick a special reading time during the day. Read all sorts of books, including nonfiction and poetry. From time to time, encourage your child to predict what a book will be about from its title and illustrations. Occasionally, discuss a book briefly after you read it.

Activities to Share

Reading List

Here are some books you and your child may enjoy. They have themes and concepts compatible with **Second Grade Scholar**.

The Busy Body Guide: A Kid's Guide to Fitness
by Lizzy Rockwell

Dear Mrs. LaRue: Letters from Obedience School
by Mark Teague

Diary of a Worm
by Doreen Cronin

How Things Work (Discovery Series)
by Alison Porter

The Magic Schoolbus at the Waterworks
by Joanna Cole

The Random House Book of Poetry for Children
collected by Jack Prelutsky

Weather (Discovery Series)
by David Ellyard

Where the Sidewalk Ends
by Shel Silverstein

Wild About Books
by Judy Sierra

Science

The Science of Sound

Help your child to make a musical instrument by wrapping a rubber band around a coffee can. Let the child pluck the rubber band and discover what happens. Your child will notice that the rubber band moves, or **vibrates**, to make a sound. Have your child experiment with six thick rubber bands stretched around a plastic box to make a "guitar." Let your child tune the guitar by tightening some of the rubber bands on the edge of the box to make different notes. Do the tightly stretched rubber bands make higher or lower notes than the untightened ones? Have your child form a theory about why the more tightly stretched rubber bands make higher notes.

Shadow Fun

Help your child make puppets by cutting outlines of people and animals out of cardboard or construction paper. Tape the puppets onto craft sticks. Hang a sheet across a doorway as a screen. You and your child stand with flashlights on one side of the sheet. Turn out the lights. Have your child hold the puppets while you shine the flashlights on them to cast a shadow on the sheet. Move the flashlights. Have your child observe that the nearer the flashlight is to the puppet, the bigger the puppet becomes. This is because as the flashlight gets nearer the puppet, the puppet blocks more light and creates a bigger shadow.

Experiment with Water

Fill two jars with water to the same level. Put the lid on one jar and leave the lid off the other. Check the jars in a few days. The jar without the lid should contain less water. Where did the water go? Let your child think about it. The only place the water could have gone was into the air. The water made the air moister.

Now have your child fill a jar with ice water. Check the jar about half an hour later. What has happened? Water drops have gathered on the outside of the glass. Where did the water drops come from? If your child guesses the air, he or she is correct. The cold air near the water glass couldn't hold as much water as warm air, so water dropped out of the air and formed on the glass.

Collections

Your child can collect interesting things from a backyard, park, or playground. Leaf collections can be made in the summer or fall. Have your child hunt for as many different kinds of leaves as possible. Tape the leaves onto pieces of paper, stack the sheets in a pile, and weight the pile with several heavy books. Consult guidebooks to identify the trees from which the leaves came.

Your child can increase his or her knowledge of geology by making a rock collection. He or she can begin by collecting small rocks and stones in the neighborhood. As you travel, your child can be on the lookout for interesting rocks, too.

Children enjoy collecting seeds. The seeds can be from produce such as watermelons, cantaloupes, apples, and peaches. You may also explore your backyard or the local park to find seeds. Your child may want to let the seeds dry, glue them to cardboard, and label them, or your child may decide to germinate and plant some of the seeds to see what kind of plant grows.

Activities to Share

Social Studies

Picture This!

Help your child take photographs of familiar places in your neighborhood, such as the grocery store, post office, gas station, fire station, and a friend's house. After the photos are printed, help your child glue them on a sheet of butcher paper to make a map of your neighborhood.

Community Workers

Talk with your child about community workers, such as checkout clerks, police officers, doctors, and teachers. Help your child set up an interview with one of these people. Let your child ask the person questions about his or her job and help the child write or tape record the answers. When you return home, have your child draw a picture of the worker and write a sentence that explains what the worker does. Encourage your child to give the worker the picture as a thank-you gift for the interview.

Family Storytelling Quilt

Tell your child a story about a family member. After you tell the story, have your child draw a portrait of that person. Hang the picture on your child's bedroom wall. As an ongoing activity, have your child draw a picture of other family members as you tell stories about them. Your child can tape the pictures together on the wall to make a family storytelling quilt. Encourage your child to retell the stories.

Eating History

Let your child help you read recipes and prepare a dish for which your area of the country is noted. For example, if you live by the water, you might prepare fish or other seafood; if you live in Iowa, you might cook a corn dish; if you live in California or Texas, you might choose tacos. As you cook with your child, discuss the importance of the food to your area and to your family.

Mathematics

The National Council of Teachers of Mathematics (NCTM) has developed the Curriculum and Evaluation Standards for School Mathematics to recommend appropriate mathematical preparation for grades K-12. These standards specify that the mathematics curriculum should emphasize problem solving, use reasoning skills, communicate about mathematics, and make connections among math topics and other subjects. It also specifies that children should learn to value mathematics and become confident in their own abilities. The NCTM advises that children have hands-on and varied experiences; use manipulatives, calculators, and computers; and work in pairs or cooperative groups.

There are many ways you can help your child accomplish the NCTM goals at home. Here are some suggestions:

Follow Up the Lessons

Follow up each math lesson with similar types of activities immediately and the next day. Help your child retain major mathematical concepts and skills by asking similar questions or thinking of similar problems. Urge him or her to talk about the problems to develop communication skills. Ask how school lessons are similar to these activities.

Math Journal

Use a notebook as a math journal. Have your child record math vocabulary words as they appear in the lessons. Review these words from time to time by talking about them and suggesting your child write about them. Have your child record interesting problems and puzzles. Ask your child to write about ways math is used every day at home, in stores, or in the neighborhood. The math journal can be taken on trips for your child to make entries about numbers on signs or buildings, record license plate numbers or time and temperature, and list ways a number can be written (10 = 4 + 6, 3 + 3 + 2 + 2, and so on). Many Try It! activities can be done in the math journal.

Math Every Day

Nurture your child's curiosity by asking a math question every day. Ask your child to help you figure out an answer to a real-life problem, such as finding the best buy or measuring something. Ask him or her about the shapes in nature and man-made things, such as boxes or buildings. Plan periodic hunts for mathematics in the home, at an event, or in the park. Involve other members of the family.

Develop Problem Solvers

Have counters handy for your child to figure out computational problems if addition or multiplication facts are not recalled easily. Use common objects, such as coins, straws, or buttons. Also help your child realize that there may be many ways to solve a problem, and that some problems have more than one solution. When your child makes a mistake, analyze the approach and information used.

Answers

Page 2

1. teacher
2. parents
3. guide
4. visitors
5. Answers will vary.

Page 3

6. carrying
7. climbs
8. starts
9. wave
10. Answers will vary.

Page 6

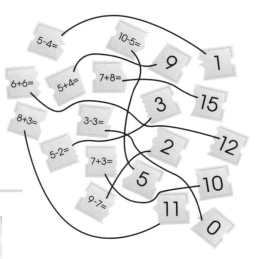

Pages 4 & 5

1. See map.
2. four
3. two
4. two
5. Places include: parks, a mall, and schools.

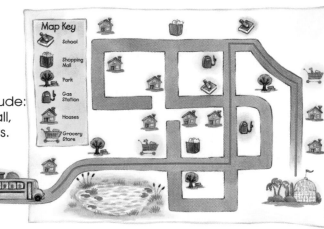

Page 7

1. There's, there + is
2. I'm, I + am
3. Here's, here + is
4. We'll, we + will or I'll, I + will
5. I'll, I + will or We'll, we + will
6. Let's, let + us

Page 8

Page 9

1. fact
2. fact
3. opinion
4. fact
5. opinion
6. opinion
7. opinion
8. fact

Page 10

p	e	i
9	6	5
+ 7	+ 5	+ 3
1. 16	2. 11	3. 8

s	H	g	c
8	9	8	5
+ 7	+ 8	+ 4	+ 4
4. 15	5. 17	6. 12	7. 9

r	h	n	i
8	6	8	6
+ 6	+ 4	+ 5	+ 2
8. 14	9. 10	10. 13	11. 8

Answer: He's chirping.

Page 11

Page 12

1. plastic
2. cans
3. paper
4. glass
5. paper
6. plastic

Page 13

Subtraction problems will vary, but differences should be the same as in each item.

Example:

Pages 16 & 17

2. <u>butterflies</u> are insects⊙

3. <u>there</u> are many kinds of butterflies⊙

4. <u>butterflies</u> live all over the world⊙

5. <u>they</u> help flowers become fruit and seeds⊙

6. <u>most</u> butterflies fly during the day⊙

7. <u>Some</u> butterflies live only a week or two⊙

8. <u>how</u> can they defend themselves ?

9. <u>some</u> make themselves stink⊙

10. <u>others</u> taste bad⊙

11. <u>yuck</u> !

12. <u>who</u> wants to be a butterfly ?

Page 21

1. green + houses
2. rain + forest
3. Every + one
4. note + books
5. back + packs
6. Some + one
7. Some + body

Page 14

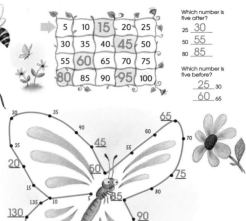

Page 18

Page 19

1. lots   spots
2. grow   slow
3. plants   ants
4. bugs   slugs
5. blow   grow
6. tall   wall

Page 22

1. hind
2. smooth
3. water
4. plump
5. bumpy
6. land

Answer: amphibians

Page 15

Which number is five after?

25 __30__
50 __55__
80 __85__

Which number is five before?

__25__ 30
__60__ 65

Page 20

$$17 - 9 = 8 \quad 16 - 8 = 8 \quad 17 - 8 = 9$$

1. 8   2. 8   3. 9

$$16 - 9 = 7 \quad 15 - 8 = 7 \quad 14 - 9 = 5$$

4. 7   5. 7   6. 5

Page 23

Answers

Pages 24 & 25

1. a kind of bird
2. too many ants
3. Quail came to live in the garden.
4. faster
5. Most children will write that bamboo grows taller.
6. Bamboo is used for houses, furniture, and other necessary things.

Page 29

Children should have drawn blossoms on cactuses 2, 3, 5, 6, and 7.

Page 33

B Martin Luther King Day, January 20

C Columbus Day, Second Monday in October

E Valentine's Day, February 14

D New Year's Day, January 1

A Independence Day, July 4

Page 26

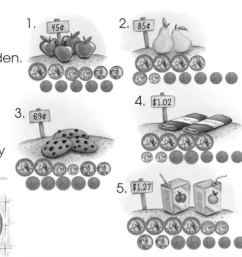

1. 45¢
2. 85¢
3. 69¢
4. $1.02
5. $1.27

Page 30

1. 25, 8, 15, 58, 36
2. Answers should include the word *cactus*.

Page 31

4 **Mosses and Ferns**
   by Eugenia Charles

3 **How Plants Grow**
   by M. E. Patinkin

1 **Amazing Seeds**
   by Janice Carson

5 **Plant Kingdoms**
   by Alice Addams

6 **Wildflowers of Michigan**
   by Henry Spinella

2 **First Seeds, Then Plants**
   by Gary Grove

Pages 34 & 35

1. See map.
2. Tropical Garden
3. rectangle
4. triangle
5. square

Page 27

1. water
2. trees
3. oil
4. fish
5. water
6. trees

Page 28

10:45

2:15

12:30

3:05

1:30

11:00

Page 32

1.
May	October
January	July
March	September

2.
November	April
December	August
June	February

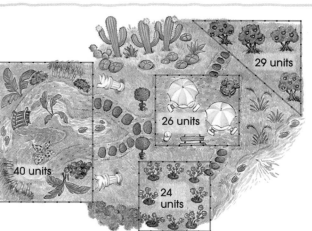

29 units

26 units

40 units

24 units

Page 36

gas
gas
liquid
solid
gas
liquid
solid

Page 37

1. 3/4 2. 1/4 3. 1/2 4. 4/6

5. 6/8 6. 2/3 7. 5/6

Page 38

Page 39

1. seeds
2. dandelions
3. trees
4. coconuts
5. classes
6. buses
7. wishes
8. teaches

Page 40

1. Cactus
2. Poison Oak
3. Orange
4. Thistle
5. Rose

Page 41

Wording of answers will vary.

1. The class has a snack.
2. Mrs. Cone's hat blows off.
3. Everyone puts on hats and scarves.
4. It gets warmer
5. A boy is missing
6. Someone gives star fruit to the class

Pages 42 & 43

Estimates will vary slightly.

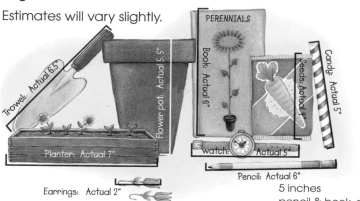

Trowel: Actual 6.5"
Flower pot: Actual 5.5"
Planter: Actual 7"
Earrings: Actual 2"
PERENNIALS
Book: Actual 6"
Seeds: Actual 4"
Candy: Actual 5"
Watch: Actual 5"
Pencil: Actual 6"
5 inches
pencil & book, candy & watch

Page 44

1. thermometer
2. tweezers
3. trowel
4. tape measure

Page 45

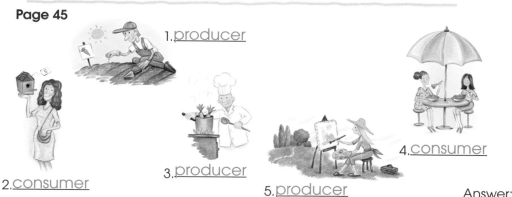

1. producer
2. consumer
3. producer
4. consumer
5. producer

Page 46

LL	VA	OR	NI
29	18	15	17
+ 3	+ 5	+ 5	+ 9
32	23	20	26

A	S	CE	O
32	16	10	17
+ 8	+ 6	+14	+ 8
40	22	24	25

DU	CH	PR	ID
15	17	15	33
+16	+24	+15	+17
31	41	30	50

Answer: ORCHIDS PRODUCE VANILLA.

Answers

Page 47

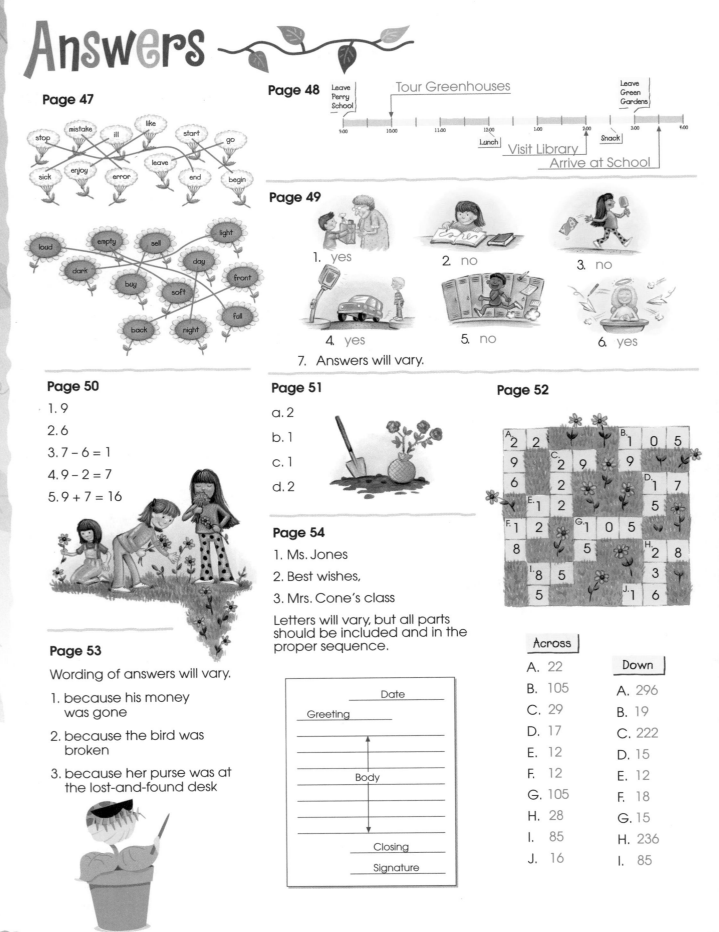

Page 48

Leave Perry School — Tour Greenhouses — Lunch — Visit Library — Arrive at School — Snack — Leave Green Gardens

(Timeline: 9:00, 10:00, 11:00, 12:00, 1:00, 2:00, 3:00, 4:00)

Page 49

1. yes
2. no
3. no
4. yes
5. no
6. yes
7. Answers will vary.

Page 50

1. 9
2. 6
3. 7 – 6 = 1
4. 9 – 2 = 7
5. 9 + 7 = 16

Page 51

a. 2
b. 1
c. 1
d. 2

Page 52

Across		Down
A. 22		A. 296
B. 105		B. 19
C. 29		C. 222
D. 17		D. 15
E. 12		E. 12
F. 12		F. 18
G. 105		G. 15
H. 28		H. 236
I. 85		I. 85
J. 16		

Page 53

Wording of answers will vary.

1. because his money was gone
2. because the bird was broken
3. because her purse was at the lost-and-found desk

Page 54

1. Ms. Jones
2. Best wishes,
3. Mrs. Cone's class

Letters will vary, but all parts should be included and in the proper sequence.

Date
Greeting
Body
Closing
Signature

Second Grade Scholar **02303**